This book is dedicated to my Grandchildren Ben,
Lizzy, Samuel, Rebecca, Isabella and Oliver
And to all the children of the World, who are
very precious to God and of whom Jesus said
'of such is the Kingdom of Heaven'

THE SAD LITTLE OYSTER

A wonderful Saviour is Jesus my Lord
A wonderful Saviour to me
He hideth my soul in the cleft of the rock
Where rivers of pleasure I see

*Chorus*
He hideth my soul in the cleft of the rock
That shadows a dry, thirsty land
He hideth my life in the depths of His love
And covers me there with His hand
And covers me there with His hand

FANNY CROSBY

Fanny Crosby (1820-1915) was blind all her life, but loved Jesus and wrote many wonderful hymns

# The Sad Little Oyster

by
Pat Greenslade

LOXWOOD PRESS

ISBN 978-1-908113-28-3

Illustrations by Livio Martinkovic, RGD, Worthing

Published by Loxwood Press, 50 Loxwood Ave, Worthing, West Sussex BN14 7RA

Printed by CZ Design & Print
Unit 3 Southmill Trading Centre
Bishop's Stortford CM23 3DY

**All proceeds from the sale of this book go to Compassion UK which works in Jesus' name to release children from poverty**

## NOTES FOR PARENTS, CARERS AND TEACHERS

Many children today suffer from low self-esteem and need to be told:

- That God loves them just as they are and has a special plan for their life.
- God has no favourites. He loves each one of them just as much as He loves everyone else.
- He loves them when they're good and He loves them when they're bad; He loves them all the time: explain age-appropriately that this is called unconditional love.
- He thinks they're special even if they don't think so.
- He wants to be their special friend.
- He wants them to tell Him all their problems.

Ollie the oyster made his home in a cleft of a rock. Jesus said that when we give our life to Him and follow His Word (the Bible), we are like a wise man who builds his house upon a rock.

Once upon a time Ollie the oyster lived in
a cleft of a rock in a beautiful
deep blue ocean.

Every morning he got out of bed and looked
in the mirror and said to himself,
“O dear, I am so ugly and I don't get any better.
I haven't even got a backbone.

All I can do is hide away inside my shell in a cleft
of a rock in this beautiful deep blue ocean.

I wish I had fins like the brightly coloured fish
swimming above me in the sea.

I wish I could escape into the warm sunshine”.

**"Why-ever did God bother to make me?"**

One day Ollie the oyster met Oscar the octopus. Oscar was very old and very wise and he quietly listened to all that Ollie had to say.

Then he said very gently, "Son, God has a special reason for making you and one day He'll show you just what it is."

Ollie waited and waited for what it
might be, but instead of getting something
nice, something horrid came along instead.

A naughty little bug named Purdy came barging
into his shell, without even being invited!
He didn't knock at the door, as any well
brought-up person would do.

He simply marched into the kitchen and
started making himself at home.
Wherever did he learn such manners!

Ollie's quiet little home just wasn't
the same any more.

He was more unhappy than ever and when
he politely asked Purdy to leave, he rudely replied,
"No I won't! This is *my* home now!"

Ollie sat down on his chair and cried and cried

"This isn't what the wise old octopus told me would happen

I'm not going to talk to him ever again!"

But of course he did and when Oscar the octopus heard all about it, he smiled a very wise old smile and said:

"Ollie, my friend, this is where God's plan for you really begins. Let me tell you what to do now

You know that beautiful shiny pearl that lines the inside of your shell?

Well, start covering Purdy with it and bit by bit you'll find that he won't bother you any more."

Day after day Ollie worked hard covering Purdy with shiny pearl; and day after day he got out of bed and looked in the mirror and said to himself:

"O dear, I am so ugly and I don't get any better; I haven't even got a backbone".

"All I can do is hide away inside my shell in a cleft of a rock in this beautiful deep blue ocean. I wish I had fins like the brightly coloured fish swimming in the sea. I wish I could escape into the warm sunshine".

**"Why ever did God bother to make me?"**

And he took no notice at all of the beautiful pearl growing inside him and he soon forgot all about Purdy.

One day when Ollie was much older, his little house started shaking and shaking and all the pots and pans in his kitchen were thrown this way and that.

He peeped out of his window and saw a deep-sea diver smiling down at him.

The diver carefully brought Ollie up to the surface and into the warm sunshine.

When Ollie's shell was gently opened, everyone stared and stared at the beautiful, shiny new pearl inside.

All the people began clapping and clapping and saying, "Ollie, what a clever little oyster you are!"

Suddenly he knew that he wasn't useless after all because God had chosen him to do a very special work for Him which even the most colourful fish in the sea could never do.

After his shell was carefully closed up again he was put back into the sea.

He hurried off to tell his friend Oscar the octopus all about his exciting adventure.

A beautiful, shiny pearl

Jesus loved children and they loved Him

In Luke 18:16 some parents brought their little children to Jesus so that He could bless them; but His disciples scolded the parents for bothering Him.

Jesus rebuked the disciples and said, "Let the children come to me. Don't stop them! For the Kingdom of God belongs to those who are like these children"

The Bible says that Jesus is our greatest treasure

In Matthew 13:45, 46 Jesus is known as 'The Pearl of Greatest Price'